Love On The Marsh
a long poem

Douglas Lochhead

Books & Chapbooks by Douglas Lochhead

The Heart is Fire *(1959)*
An old woman looks out on Gabarus Bay ... *(1959)*
It Is All Around *(1960)*
Shepherds Before Kings *(1963)*
Poet Talking *(1964)*
A & B & C &: An Alphabet *(1969)*
Millwood Road Poems *(1970)*
Prayers in a Field: Ten Poems *(1974)*
The Full Furnace: Collected Poems *(1975)*
High Marsh Road *(1980)*; *in Italian,* La Strada di Tantramar *(2004)*
A&E *(1980)*, A&E. *rev. ed. (1998)*
Battle Sequence Poems *(1980)*
The Panic Field: Prose Poems *(1984)*
Tiger in the Skull: New and Selected Poems *(1986)*
The Red Jeep and Other Landscapes *(1987)*
Upper Cape Poems *(1989)*
Dykelands (With Thaddeus Holownia) *(1989)*
Black Festival: A Long Poem *(1991)*
Homage to Henry Alline and Other Poems *(1992)*
Charlie, Boo Boo, Nutley Clutch and others *(1997)*
Breakfast at Mel's and Other Poems of Love and Places *(1997)*
All Things Do Continue: Poems *(1997)*
Millwood Road Poems *(1998)*
The Lucretius Poems *(1998)*
Cape Enrage: Poems on a Raised Beach *(2000)*
Yes, Yes, Yes! *(2001)*
Orkney: October Diary *(2002)*
Weathers: Poems New & Selected *(2002)*
Midgic *(2003)*
That Place by Tantramar: Sackville, New Brunswick *(2007)*
Love on the Marsh *(2008)*

Love On The Marsh
a long poem

Douglas Lochhead

SYBERTOOTH INC
SACKVILLE, NEW BRUNSWICK

Litteris Elegantis Madefimus

Ki no Tsurayuki's "as the waters of Yodo Marsh" (poem 587) from
Kokinshū: A Collection of Poems Ancient and Modern, translated and
annotated by Laurel Rasplica Rodd with Mary Catherine Henkenius
(Princeton: Princeton University Press, 1984 / Boston: Cheng & Tsui
Co., 1996) reprinted by kind permission of Laurel Rasplica Rodd.

First published 2008 by   Sybertooth Inc.
59 Salem Street
Sackville, NB
E4L 4J6
Canada
www.sybertooth.ca

The paper in this edition is acid free
and meets all ANSI standards for archival quality.

Library and Archives Canada Cataloguing in Publication

Lochhead, Douglas, 1922-
Love on the marsh : a long poem / Douglas Lochhead.

ISBN 978-0-9739505-3-3

I. Title.

PS8523.O33L68 2008 C811'.54 C2007-907577-0

to all lovers

as the waters of
Yodo Marsh   where they reap the
   true reeds   swell and flood
when the long rains fall   my heart
fills with ever-growing love

Ki no Tsurayuki

1.

the marsh:
this is our stage
wide green place
of discovery, of love,
of venturing into caves
where clouds live.

2.

it began with your eyes. bouquet
of two. daisies along the path.
beyond was the sea. summer's fires
were everywhere. petals of love
flew on the marsh wind.
backyard Eden.
this is our place.

3.

forgive me before we say anything.
will we wait for the night? what
do your arms say? I am stranger.
we are young. there are questions.
do you hear me?

4.

the reaching, touching poet.
love lopes in many ways. it is
that splendour of many paths.
it spreads in its curving ways
across the marsh. my love, let's
follow. these are beginnings.

5.

there are decisions. I await
your elucidations. your stolid
one-liners which reach around
this place. the sky as blackboard.
a message of clouds.

6.

take me. take me into your wide
embrace. what are we here for?
you ask. hey, we are here to
celebrate. spell it, please.
L - O - V - E.

7.

sky, marsh, the setting.
how to begin? how to spell
love? stay a while and in our
arms we will ponder this.
such a wide, green bed.

8.

today I am prisoner.
sequestered on the rack. is
that the word? take me, I cry.
forget the whips. let me tell
my story. we are explorers.
let us break out.

9.

there are times when I want
to shout for help. the deep and
desperate need is there.
am I alone in this?

10.

the daily assembly. life
is put and held together.
the parts take over.
let us be surgeons
for each other.
let us go inside
ourselves.

11.

last night a parade of dreams.
crazy corners of never places.
forgotten. what curious
currents drive this way and
that. but it was a parade
in which I marched.
you were there.

12.

today, into my kitchen, a
sculpture from the Metropolitan
Museum of Art. cycladic figure,
a woman in stone on tip-toe.
'abstract geometrical' but
a woman who stands in the kitchen.
it is a marked day on my
calendar.

13.

when alone I harbour
two handfuls of leaves.
to throw them into air means
a laugh, a kick, a second
of wildness. a shower over
the road and marsh.
may they fall into your lap.

14.

the contest of winds. more
messages. take me tonight
into your arms. God will
listen in good time. we
must have a chat about this.
with God I mean.

15.

clouds become faces. they
have their own messages.
I should take more time
to watch. to listen.

16.

today there are new tears.
the barn door of loneliness creaks
open. it is a new blackness.
is there a flower waiting
somewhere in the dark?

17.

today I ask one question:
where are your arms?

18.

the dirty mountains of February
are all around. no rain. our lips
fail. the path (the road) leads
nowhere. we have each other.

19.

the forever marsh blown with hard
snow. along the ditch black stems
of dead weeds. held to the light
their outlines tell of diamonds.
thorns against the sky. whose face
is mine?

20.

new tears I admit. now the searing
search for new words.

21.

marsh. I lie in you face down.
to listen. it is for signals we wait.
come signals let me read you.

22.

walk with me. I know you are out
there. we know each other too well.
no need to worry. there will be
no questions. it will kill me
but I want you.

23.

because of this I am drunk.
sorrow is my drink.

24.

is every day a sentimental journey?
what does the road say? questions
lie along the fence. answers fly
as crows on the changing winds.
out there.

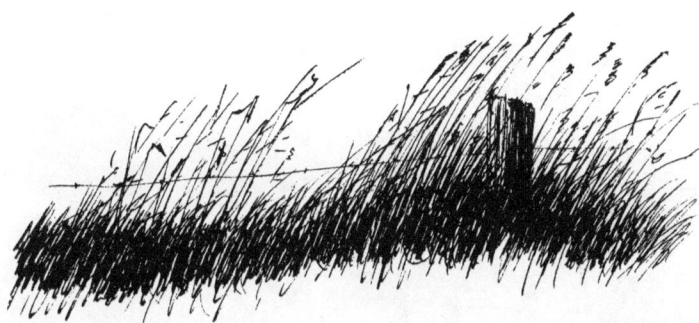

25.

the poem takes over. it is between
us. one gives thanks. the right
words wait. I listen for your tune.
should I?

26.

parts of you, your body, come to me.
over the stretch of sea out there.
my hand between your legs. yours
between mine. we look into each
others eyes.

27.

you are the forest. the apple hills.
landscape of silk. you know what
I am talking about.

28.

what happened? when? love-boat sinking.
Captain! there is need of rescue.
God's arms will take us.
Let us pray.

29.

just a phone call. just. it goes on.
the voice echoes and plays. sleep
hell. is this the thinning of love?
the final descent?

30.

the old saviour. marsh road. this day
the sky has no messages. it is
simply there. it is a waiting place
for intensive care.

31.

do I exaggerate? a parade of pain
with marching bands. take me from all
this. do not give in. tug-of-war.
love's umbilical. stand fast!

32.

the search is for tracks.
waiting is my name. the road
is moist with April.

33.

listen. who has heard laughter?
questions fall in the wind like
loose slates. there are signs.
a kind of danger.

34.

today a wide blue sky. over Shepody
a distant fling of cloud. fish scales.
it is a swath. *cirrocumulus undulatus*.

35.

beginnings all around. but are they
beginnings? a long poem lies some-
where out there. wait. wait for it.
we will find parts.
we will put them together.

36.

listen. the voice of the wind.
it tells a story. let us hear
the old refrain. it is
the story of love.

37.

listen to the past. flakes of memory.
funny faces in the mirror. one way
to erase the blahs of the season.
loneliness. the curse of it.

38.

it is the Goose Lake Road.
in the year two barns blown down.
wind smashed. what forces. timbers,
rafters and shingles taken away.
the farmers have burned the old
floors. cleansed.

39.

not unlike the "Our Father..."
Prayer. a new version is needed.
an exile's. I happened on it years ago.
it is all around. love, of course.
all around this marsh.

40.

let me begin: "your presence is
all around, hallowed be God's name…"
we are listening. we are learning.
our knees in the marsh mud.

41.

more lessons. more times on the
marsh. do we go together as lovers?
as someone said: "I don't think so."
but someone is wrong. we are
here and the soft wind tells
of our learning passion.

42.

coming here is a celebration.
a ceremony. the hay is greener
when we look into its eyes.
love in a place.

43.

yes, the need to celebrate. every-
thing. even the day-long noise
of the crows. count what they are
saying. caw, caw. ha ha.

44.

today the road is a corridor.
shaped thoughts. griefs are company
in the tunnelled place.
someone's silence can do it.

45.

why? today we are not alone.
over this marsh through shivering
grasses ran Jonathan Eddy, the big
boy from Maine and elsewhere. Colonel
Eddy was out to capture the fort.
Beausejour. 1776

46.

we are all young. we are all old.
look at the new hay. the bent stalks.
it is all a growing thing. we are
in each other's arms.

47.

wide company of clouds. up there
over Minudie. I salute them. happy
with this day of sun. but the forecasts
say rain, heavy at times. it will
be reflected in the eyes and words
at the post office.

48.

Eddy is here again. fast Eddy ghost.
I see him doing the leopard crawl
through marsh hay. over to the right
is his GAP. Shepody mountain. Eddy
urging on his mixed bag of
marauders.

49.

a poem tumbles out of the sky.
no chute. the immediate task is to
drag it in. come to me my love.
from me come a lover's directions.
what will the mole and the mouse say?
anything for a poem.

50.

it came to me this morning. there
are no beginnings. now that is
something to play with. proof is
all around. we will make lists.
a short list emerges.
our only word is love.

51.

this day a welcome of dandelions.
I sat on Mr. Trueman's edge. Have
you ever given time to a dandelion?
we will look into its eyes.

52.

the susurrous of the new hay.
summer music, summer wind of
sadness. remember Frank Sinatra.
summer wind.

53.

only the hard rhythm of each day.
the nimble darting panoply of pain.
you ought to be grateful it is not
worse. think of old, yes old, so and so.
tell me about it, he said, yes,
counting the ways he would be told,
taking out the old chuckle he saved
for much looking out of windows.

54.

a heron leans with the sound.
where the land leaks with sea.
it is a set place. another beginning.
let us take new wings.

55.

lessons. marsh as mother. her wide
apron covers the place.
we will listen to her words.
then go our own way.
two together.

56.

so. a question. do you hear me?
it is about love. the sea's pleasure.
let us sit together on this log.
the sea has answers for us.

57.

the expedition is preparing. there is
a marching off in many directions.
time for an O group. it will take
a few days to locate the enemy. this
march is inward.

58.

I feel like a leopard crawl with my love.
she has a plan. I have mine. what is
distance between when there is love?

59.

there is something alive in the clouds.
in the wind's song. the billows are
close comfort on an otherwise empty stage.
we are learning. aren't we?

60.

in the clouds there are many faces.
together they are love's portrait. I
seem to recognize the figure, the stance,
the face.

61.

today I found a crow feather. almost a
foot long. black beauty. what is its story?
we stand no chance of telling it.

62.

definitions: we reach for them.
hands. fingers on the horizon's edge.
what winds blow? we topple on the
rim and fall in.

63.

the poem takes over. one gives
thanks. the right words wait out
there. they play part of the game.
yes, your tune will do.

64.

a playing field of love. well
named. time leaks over it all.
let us come together to toss
a coin, to spin our lucky dice.

65.

the marsh, this our playground.
we agree. it is all a game of
sorts. rules. who are the
referees? let us love the wind,
its constancy.

66.

lips and love. our warm breath
growing on marsh wind. do your
tortured parts feel my urge? do
we begin to talk at last?

67.

the wild and warm dance. it
takes us into its arms. what
is the crazy step, or steps,
we would take?

68.

late it is. the marsh grass
is a table of darkness. let us
go into the green summer depths.
let us explore them. and ourselves.
I know you will greet the great
silence.

69.

find me. hide me. take me.
full and frequent. love lies
on the counter of life. give
me more.

70.

we are all in love. on the blue
and quivering truth. a sharing.
a loud lick of love. a laugh
and the world is undone.

71.

whenever, wherever there is
a beginning. let it be love.
each word. each embrace
leading to warm beginnings.
yes, yes, yes!

72.

the running mystery of your lips.
their moist touch, their sounds.
what words do I believe? tell me
with your lips. the marsh is wet
with waiting.

73.

take it from here. again the kissing
bridge. time is always right.
look through. will you watch
with me the sunrise?

74.

the hard measures of the marsh.
love's long universal migraine.
there is opposition from the stars.
do you remember that night of pain?

75.

let us shake on it. no,
that is too remote. crazy
ritual. agreement of what?
the whole thing lies face down
on the marsh.

76.

'Beauty thou fantastik ape,'
so sang Abraham Cowley. beauty
and love go together. love leaps
and swings from the branches. it
laughs and cries even on the marsh.
fantastik!

77.

the month of May. a green taking.
a harrier plots new ground. a
fresh wind of spring warmth. how
much of all love is plotting,
is taking?

78.

to go back. back from where?
the road is a beginning, an
ending. they are one. and the
same. as with everything. now
take love.

79.

love. a delicate sharing. a
putting on of hands.
there is more to say.
we each have a story.

80.

blame rhymes with shame.
you have made your list.
is that your portrait of me?

81.

there is no time for ill-will.
so much for the morning phone call
cancelling everything. there is
a certain feeling of relief.
it will flower again.

82.

signs. eyes squander their limits.
life is an unveiling. the unprobed
edges lose what definition there
was. there is sad music of breaking
waves.

83.

out there beyond marsh is the sea.
its splendid margins of change.
its measurements of sail. the
deep closures of the tide.

84.

our love goes on again.
as we walk along the road
we lift the blanket of green.
the marsh undoes itself
and takes us in. it is
the place for all lovers.

85.

look,
out there burns a summer fire.
more green flames in the wide garden.
whose fields unfold around us?
there are limits we must reach for.
we begin again at the edge. here.

86.

everything begins and ends in fire.
we bring our own embers.
it is a sharing. love lingers here.
and here. it is all around.

87.

now is night. it opens its far limits
and reveals the marsh. seeds are secrets.
there is smoke. it breeds change.
our love holds.

88.

there are late dancers. they laugh
and cavort. they are married
to the wind. something almost wild
blows in from the sea. flags of love.

89.

a question:
who has made the arrangements?
you and I, my love, must join hands
and search the sky. look, hay bales
form a temple. there is
green light from those green fires.

90.

the build-up is from here.
we are a spark. a candle shimmers.
the bed of love surrounds us.
life is many expeditions.
let us meet again at the kissing bridge.

91.

look over the marsh.
a long traffic of clouds.
con un fuerte abrazo
yes, a thousand embraces.

92.

a hymn of joy from the lips
of angels. it overflows the marsh.
the cup is in your hand. please
share it with me.
to live, to share, to love.

93.

at the edge. here we are.
let us take to our knees.
the marsh is God's church.
a prayer-place for lovers.
we must find words. yes, love.

94.

teach us, God, to live together
in your night's seasons.
to see in each other's eyes
the lively passion of your life.

95.

teach me the strange language
of the aged. let me translate it
for my love. this is my story.
to be spread wide on the marsh.

96.

we feel the long reach of love.
fields of hay a soft bed.
the marsh road is a reminder.
an escort of daisies runs
along the ditch. white faces smile.

97.

we follow the marsh road.
it is our bridal place.
a slow march together.
as two, as one, always
as lovers.

98.

my words are yours.
yours carry me everywhere.
the green place marries the blue.
our world is this road of love
our world becomes the sky.

99.

yes, it is, the long limb of love.
the road again across the marsh.
there are no worry stones
for fingers to embrace
only your arms and mine
which we agree are enough.

100.

our venturing, our passion,
our lovers' fire. what words,
what music fills the air.
it is a ceremony, a celebration
amid this wide kingdom.
God provides the final embrace.
love is everywhere.
listen, it is the heartbeat of God.

Other books published by Sybertooth Inc.
www.sybertooth.ca

~~~~~~

The Canvas Barricade
by Donald Jack

In print for the first time, Donald Jack's comedy *The Canvas Barricade* was the first modern play performed on the main stage of the Stratford Festival (1961).

Misty Woodenbridge, a painter, has rejected the materialism of modern society for life in a tent by the Ottawa River, where he lives as carefree as the fabled grasshopper, eating stolen apples and painting masterpieces. But as summer draws to an end, reality rears its ugly head, and Misty must choose between starving in his tent and moving to the city with his fiancée. Meanwhile, his in-laws-to-be smell a cash cow when a mysterious art buyer begins snapping up Misty's work – and naturally they keep the money. Out of kind consideration for Misty's artistic ideals, of course...

ISBN-10: 0968802494 • ISBN-13: 9780968802496
Trade paperback, published 2007
£12.00 • $16.00

~~~~~~

Beyond Window-Dressing?
Canadian Children's Fantasy at the Millennium
by K.V. Johansen

Recipient of the IBBY Canada 2004 Frances E. Russell Award for research in children's literature.

In the late twentieth century, Canadian children's fantasy had a poor reputation internationally. Was this reputation deserved, and if so, has the quality of children's fantasy and the climate for its publication improved since that time? After a survey of twentieth-century Canadian children's fantasy, *Beyond Window-Dressing* examines these questions through an extensive cross-section of Canadian children's fantasy published between 2000 and 2004. *Beyond Window-Dressing* provides not only a window onto Canadian developments in the genre during the opening years of the twenty-first century, but insists that fantasy must be judged by standards as rigorous as those applied to any other genre of literature.

~~~~~~

And from Donald Jack's classic, triple Leacock Medal winning historical fiction series
The Bandy Papers

It's Me Again: *Volume III of The Bandy Papers*
ISBN-10: 097395051X • ISBN-13: 9780973950519
Trade paperback • published 2007
£12.00 • $16.00

Me So Far: Volume VII of The Bandy Papers
ISBN: 9780973950502
Trade paperback • published 2007
£12.00 • $16.00

Hitler Versus Me: *Volume VIII of the Bandy Papers*
(includes the novelette 'Where Did Rafe Madison Go?')
ISBN-10: 0968802486 • ISBN-13: 9780968802489
Trade paperback • published 2006
£12.00 • $16.00

Stalin Versus Me: *Volume IX of The Bandy Papers*
ISBN-10: 0968802478 • ISBN-13: 9780968802472
Trade paperback • published 2005
£12.00 • $16.00

~~~~~~

Also From Sybertooth Inc.

Quests and Kingdoms
A Grown-Up's Guide to Children's Fantasy Literature
By K.V. Johansen
462pp • $30.00 • £20.00 • Trade paperback 2005
ISBN-10: 0968802443 • ISBN-13: 9780968802441
Shortlisted for the 2006 Harvey Darton Award

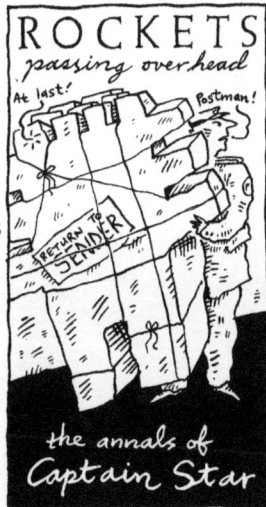